Words On Paper

Jazmine greene

BookLeaf
Publishing

India | USA | UK

Presentation by *BookLeaf Publishing*

Web: www.bookleafpub.com

E-mail: info@bookleafpub.com

ISBN: 9789358312423

First edition 2023

To my family who always pushed me to always be writing. To my family who isn't blood and yet always supported me and listen to my tales. My best friend who at times edited my writing even without me asking. These people hold a dear place in my heart. They have listened to me talk about my writing and read my poetry.

A conversation with my Muse

The Muse
Well well I figured it's about time that you and I
spoke
You're writing more consistently than usual. I
am proud of you
So please tell me what I can do for you. How
can I assist you at this very moment?

Me
I want to thank you for being my constant guide
to my creative writing my poetry to my soul
Through everything in my life, you have been
one of the constant things that are there
Even when I couldn't write you were still in the
back of my head giving me the things I need
I am forever in your debt. My beautiful muse

The Muse
My dear poet
I guide you because you have this gift
That you must share with the world that you
have to share within yourself
I will forever be with you
I will forever be around you

I will live in the things you love
I will live in the things that make me happy
I live in things that make me sad
I will forever be in your soul

Here are some things I want you to remember
Always keep writing
Always be creative
This is who you are
And by damn you will never forget that
My dear friend, this is your life
You are a writer

Pain is different

My pain is different from others
Internalized it
Wrote about it
Had breakdowns
Self-harmed

Internalized
Eventually, it began to eat me alive
I took it and kept it

To burden others was something
I couldn't do

Who could I trust?
Who would listen?
Would anyone care?

I wrote about it
Poetry was the best form of expressing myself
To convey words in different ways in a new
poem
But in some way, they all connected

Breakdowns
That was something new

An overwhelming need to cry and cry
Self-hating
Self-deprecating
No one can hurt me
because I hurt myself so much more

Self Harm
I understand and know it's not ok
It's unhealthy, unsafe

There is part of me that doesn't care
I merely detach
To feel this release
To be in control

To feel what I think is free
A razor to my skin
So l cut and cut and cut
I'm fully aware I'm not ok
I cry and I cut and I'm done
That feeling is deep within me
Wanting to feel that pain
Longing for its sensation
To have those tears
To have that detachment

My pain is different from others
My pain isn't what it was years ago
My pain has grown

My pain has molded

I'm learning from my pain to better from it
To be truly free from it

look inward

We expect so much from others
Why don't we expect that in ourselves
potential and aspirations are something that we
should have within us
We can expect others to be great
You can't expect others to show up
When we can't even show for ourselves
Maybe a little self-reflection
Can change that

Impulsive thoughts

I wonder what it is like to die
Then come back
To know what it feels like to open the car door
And fall out
Put my whole palm down
On a hot stove

Speak the first thing on my mind
Have no filter

To punch a person in the face of whom
I don't like

To jump off a cliff into a body of water
And see what happens

Allow me to truly remember
To let myself actually feel
What's inside

Walls

I have barriers around me I know where they
came from
to think or to act as if I didn't know is foolish
Even those whom I love
I share these walls with
I don't know if it's because I can't trust people
fully
and I know deep deep down that I should be able
to
but there's this part of me that won't
I don't know how to begin to truly show who I
am even those who I love dear
Been carrying these walls as my barriers for
most of my life
how do I begin
where do I start

Loneliness

It either can be your saving grace
Or
It can be your damnation

In our loneliness
We need to dig deep to find who we are
Exploring parts of us that people haven't seen
yet

Face who truly are and learn to accept
Or
Change to be something better

Other Places

Home sometimes isn't a place
It can be a person

If you're lucky that person
Will hold on to you
Will fight for you
Be the one

Loves sometimes isn't a person
It can be so many things

You can find love in your career
In your passions
In all the small joys in life
At times in things you least expected

Happiness sometimes isn't guaranteed
Happiness is something you look for
Happiness is something you fight for

Life is life

Life is hard

Life is death

Life is living

Home sometimes isn't a place
It can be in you

What you smell

Have you ever just smelled something
that just made you look back
For me
I didn't know where I was going
Or what I was seeking
but I had this feeling coming over with me
that felt utterly sensational

I don't know if I have smelled this before
or experienced something with that scent

I don't know if I should be worried that I don't
remember
or be grateful for the fact that I don't remember
memories are quite tricky

Could I create a new memory with this new
scent?

Am I reading too much in doing that smell?

Tripping,Fallling

There are things that I don't understand
 how can one day you see someone one way
 then in some strange way, you see them
 completely different
 the way they walk
 the way they talk
  the way they look
  then eventually you solely fall for them more
and more

I drift off and when I'm drifting you're with me
 when I think of what I want you are always
there

You're who I want to kiss
Your who I want to share a life with

You live in every being of me
 I cannot shake you
 I cannot stop thinking of you

It's like a dream that I wish to never forget
 I know this for sure I don't understand where
this came from
 I accept it

and sooner or later move on from what I feel
sometimes we trip
But damn I'm pretty sure I've fallen

Openminded

There are stories I wish to create
Tells and fables
Of worlds greater than is

There are visions I wish to show
Of light and dark
Beauty and ugly
Truth and lies

I need to take you on a journey
A ride of every emotion

I hope you will open your mind
And maybe understand something
Different
New

Giving Away

We give pieces of ourselves
To loved ones
To our jobs
To the hobbies we learn
To the hatred we keep
The hope we seek
Is there a chance
That we could end up
Having nothing
Left to give?

Unfinished/Finished Poems

Ramblings of parts of poems I never finished

Need a little love to ease the pain
Need a little muse to inspire creativity

Darkness has a way of creeping up on us
Maybe from the inside
Or when the day becomes the night

Sometimes we can't help who we fall in love
And at points in our lives
The people who we are close to may
Cause us pain

You gotta live your life to the fullest

I can feel it in my bones
It's in my heart
Wraps around my soul

Bound

I am bound to you
I'm bound to the idea of the possibilities of what
could be

There are these moments when times
Seemingly stops

The reality of what I desire
Plays through the mind

In that space
Unspoken realities become truth

Heart to Heart

I wasn't ready to tell you what I felt
I don't think you were ready for it yet
I'm ready to lay out everything on the table
all the emotions
The truth
This I can no longer hide
I am ready to completely show you who I'm am

So when you are ready
you come to me and you tell me
who you are
what you feel
Everything is in your court

The Show

What we tell ourselves
What we tell others
and what people think

Should we care what people think?

Putting on a show
Who's watching? Everyone
The audience is you
the critic is me
my performance deserves
a standing ovation

Maybe even an Academy Award

You're drawn to every word I say.

I speak of truth, lies
I will let you guess what is actual

Every action I make
you all become taken in
I thrive off my performance

Fools I will make of you

Many know my show is not real
Numerous are conned by my act.
I will only know
My real Truth

From Friends to More And then…And

From Friends to More And then…

Not thinking it would happen again
She confesses her feelings again
Not knowing sooner or later
That it could change like before
Understanding why it happen last time
But this time has no clue
One day they talk the next
Silence
She knew deep down
It would happen again
Ignoring what she already knew would happen
She listens to her heart instead of her head

As time passes she calls, text
Nothing
Days became weeks
Weeks became a month
She was overcome with questions

That he could not answer

Why

That's all she wants to know

Why

They were friends
They were in a relationship
He made her happy

He deleted her from his friend's list
He stops talking here

Left heartbroken

And Then...10 years

We reconnected after years of silence
He was going through a divorce
And I was desperately looking for a change

We talked for a bit
Caught up on life

He wanted a roommate
And I was happy to be obliged

A couple of months later I moved in
It was new
It was exciting

He told me he loved
He wanted to start dating

And so we did.

I was weary
I was doubtful

He broke a part of me a long time ago

So that trust wasn't there

It was rushed
I played into it
What does that make me?
I couldn't bring myself
To truly fall again
Not again

I ended that part of the relationship
There was awkwardness but eventually, it passed

Time has passed
We were still roomies

He wanted to try again
He thought we fit well together

Thinking this was what I wanted
What I needed
Underneath I knew it wasn't
I played along again
That was a shit thing to do

I moved
We talked

Then we stopped
Its life

Giving false hope to a person knowing damn
well
That the person isn't who you truly want to be
with
is wrong
It's sad
So damn disrespectful
I'm sorry

Hurt people hurt

He hurt me
I hurt him

It wasn't intentional that wasn't my plan
I didn't know how to communicate
What I truly needed or wanted
Hell I didn't even know at the time
And as I write this I'm still trying
To figure it out

Practice what you Speak

Creating stories in the mind
Practicing what I want to tell you
Playing out every scenario
That could be possible
Every honesty

Every deceit
What lies beneath
Unraveling layers upon layers
Of the human existence
To find what is heavy within the soul

Looking Back

Do you look back on your writings?

I have found some of my old poems
That I have written

It's strange because some of what I wrote
Feels like a stranger
Attach to a shadow of who I used to be

Growing and changing is life

Looking back seeing what was an all-knowing
Reading what I have written is as far as I shall
go
I will dip my toe in the pool of who it was
But I will be damn sure to be swimming in new
waters
Of me

High

Welcome to My High
it is rather freeing at times
I'm feeling stories
these thoughts
Ideas
then I just sit with it all of it
it's suffocating me but there is no death
An Ignition of Creativity

Release

Go to lay down your burdens
To yourself
Then
Your people
Whatever god you believe in

Go talk to the ones you trust
Those ones who have your back
No matter what

If you have no one
Go try and seek that salvation
Because keeping all that in will eat you alive

All those burdens will manifest into so much
pain, sadness even death

Sometimes creativity but it's not worth it

But please be cautious not everyone has your
best interest at heart
It is not easy by any means but please by any
means
Unburden yourself

Your soul will thank you later